Mo:

man of God

A book of 30 Bible readings and notes
to help you worship and pray

Tony Phelps-Jones

Published by Scripture Union, 207–209 Queensway, Bletchley, MK2 2EB, England.
Email: info@scriptureunion.org.uk
Internet: www.scriptureunion.org.uk

© Copyright all editions Causeway PROSPECTS
First published in 2006
ISBN 1 84427 219 2

The right of Causeway PROSPECTS to be identified as owning this work has been asserted by their director Tony Phelps-Jones in accordance with the Copyright, Designs and Patents Act 1988.

Causeway PROSPECTS is a division of PROSPECTS for People with Learning Disabilities and their address is PO Box 351, Reading, RG30 4XQ. Phone 0118 9516 978. Email causeway@prospects.org.uk

About Causeway Prospects: Causeway PROSPECTS provides resource materials and training to equip churches for effective outreach and ministry among people with learning disabilities. It also runs holiday weekends and special ministry at Spring Harvest and the Keswick Convention.

British Library Cataloguing-in-Publication Data: a catalogue record for this book is available from the British Library.

Scripture portions are taken from The Holy Bible: English Version for the Deaf (published as the Easy-to-Read Version) © 2000 by the World Bible Translation Center, Inc. and used with permission. Internet: www.wbtc.com

Icons © Widgit Software Ltd 2002, developed by the Rebus Symbol Development Project, designed by Cate Detheridge and used with kind permission.

Cover design by David Lund Design: www.davidlund-design.com

Internal page layout by Creative Pages: www.creativepages.org.uk

Printed and bound in Great Britain by goodmanbaylis, The Trinity Press, Worcester, UK.

Scripture Union is an international charity working with churches in more than 130 countries providing resources to bring the good news about Jesus Christ to children, young people and families – and to encourage them to develop spiritually through the Bible and prayer. As well as a network of volunteers, staff and associates who run holidays, church-based events and school Christian groups, we produce a wide range of publications and support those who use our resources through training programmes.

Using this book

 Moses, man of God and the other titles in this series are intended to help you to worship and pray. On each page there is a reading from the Bible, some thoughts and a prayer.

 The readings are from the *Easy-to-Read Version* (ETRV), a very clear and simple translation of the Bible. The reading printed each day is quite short. A longer reading is also given if you would like to read more using your own Bible. There is a list of key words and their meanings near the back of the book.

Reading the Bible

The Bible, which is sometimes called the Word of God, is not really one book but a whole library of many books. The 66 books were written by many people who God spoke to at different times. At the front of the Bible you will find a list of the titles of all the books in the Bible and the page number where each book begins.

To help you find your way around such a big book, little groups of one or two sentences have been numbered, and then groups of those sentences have been collected into chapters.

So how do you find the one or two sentences that you want in the Bible? Let's say you want to find Matthew 5:5,6. That means you need to look in the book called Matthew, in chapter number 5 and verses 5 and 6.

You can find Matthew in the list of books at the front of the Bible. This tells you which page Matthew starts on. When you have turned to the beginning of Matthew you then search for chapter 5. Look down the page until you see the numbers 5 and 6. Those are the sentences (or verses) that you need.

When you do your Bible reading, try to spend a few extra minutes praying and worshipping. Praying is talking and listening to God. You can do this aloud or without using words. You can pray on your own or with friends. Worship is telling God how much you love him, through words or songs, or things you do. This can be singing in church, but it's a lot more than that. It's about enjoying the wonderful world God has made. It's about how we speak to each other. It's about how we live our lives.

As you pray you can:

 thank God for his goodness and his help;

 tell God how great he is, and that you love him;

 ask God to help you, your friends, your family and other people.

If you are a helper using this book with someone who does not read, you will find guidance notes at the end.

The *Easy-to-Read Version* of the Bible is available to buy from Causeway PROSPECTS.

Moses, man of God

1   Meet Moses

**There was a man from the family of Levi.
He married a woman who was also from
the family of Levi. The woman became
pregnant and gave birth to a baby boy.**
Exodus 2:1,2 (Full reading Exodus 1:1,6,7; 2:1,2)

Moses was born in Egypt, near the river Nile.
Moses was a Jew, part of the Jewish people called
Israelites. The people of Israel were being
treated badly by the people of Egypt. There
were so many Israelites that the Egyptians were
afraid of them. The Egyptians thought the
Israelites would fight against them.

This book, (*Moses, man of God*) will show us how
God used Moses to lead the Israelites out of
Egypt. It took a long time. But in the end the
Israelites got to the place God wanted them to
be – called the Promised Land.

**Dear God, as I learn about the life of
Moses, please help me also to learn some
important lessons for my own life. Amen.**

2 Why Egypt?

**Jacob (Israel) travelled to Egypt with his sons.
Each son had his own family with him ...
There was a total of 70 people ...**
Exodus 1:1,5 (Full reading Exodus 1:1–5)

The country of Israel is named after a man called
Israel. Israel had 12 sons. Each son had a tribe
or family named after him. One of the sons was
called Levi. Moses came from the family of Levi.

There was no food in the country where Israel
and his family were living. So they all moved to
Egypt where there was plenty of food. One of
Israel's sons, Joseph, was the prime minister there.
You can read the story of Joseph in Genesis,
starting at chapter 37.

**There are still countries today where the
people have little or no food to eat. Ask
God to give people in African countries the
food and water they need each day.**

3   Changing times

**Then a new king began to rule Egypt ...
This king said to his people ... 'We must
make plans to stop the Israelites from
growing stronger. If there is a war, the
people of Israel might join our enemies ... '**
Exodus 1:8–10 (Full reading Exodus 1:6–10)

When the people of Israel first went to Egypt,
everybody was happy. The Israelites had
somewhere to live, the Egyptians didn't mind
them living there, and there was plenty to eat.
But then things began to change.

As years went by, the Israelite families got bigger.
At last there were so many people that the
Egyptians started to be afraid of them.

Is there a change happening in your life that is
difficult for you?

**Lord Jesus, please help me to cope well
with changes going on around me. Please
give your peace to me, my family and
friends. Amen.**

4 Being treated badly

The Egyptians forced the Israelites to work harder and harder. But the more the people of Israel were forced to work, the more they grew and spread. And the Egyptian people became more and more afraid of the people of Israel.
Exodus 1:12 (Full reading Exodus 1:11–14)

The people of Egypt started to be nasty to the people of Israel, making them work harder and harder for no money. They were slaves. The Israelites had to make bricks and build lots of houses. It was not fair.

Do you know someone who is being treated badly? God is not pleased when that happens. Is there anything you could do or say to make things better?

Dear God, please help my friend (say their name) and anyone else who is being treated badly. Amen.

5   Save the children

The king said, 'You will continue to help the Hebrew [Israelite] women give birth to their children. If a girl baby is born, then let the baby live. But if the baby is a boy, then you must kill him!'
Exodus 1:16 (Full reading Exodus 1:15–17)

The king of Egypt was really nasty to the Israelites. 'Kill the baby boys!' he said. You can't get much nastier than that, can you? He wanted to stop the Israelites from getting any more men who might later attack them.

People who are nasty to children are doing a very bad thing. We should be kind and gentle to children and look after them well.

Lord Jesus, thank you for children, especially for the children I know. Please protect them from being hurt. Help them to grow up knowing you. Amen.

6 When in danger

The woman became pregnant and gave birth to a baby boy ... After three months, she made a basket and covered it with tar so that it would float. She put the baby in the basket. Then she put the basket in the river in the tall grass.
Exodus 2:2,3 (Full reading Exodus 2:1–4)

This is a very dangerous time for baby Moses. At home he might be killed by soldiers. So his mother put him in the river in a basket. That was dangerous too. He might be killed by an animal or swept away by the river.

People today are often in danger. Maybe you or someone you know has to make a long journey. Perhaps you heard about a disaster on the news.

Dear God, I pray for anyone today who is in danger. Please keep them safe. Thank you. Amen.

7 Answer to prayer

Just then, Pharaoh's daughter went to the river to bathe ... [She] opened the basket and saw a baby boy. The baby was crying and she felt sorry for it.
Exodus 2:5,6 (Full reading Exodus 2:5–9)

The plan worked perfectly. Baby Moses was found by the king's daughter. The king's daughter asked Moses' mother to look after him for a while. Then the king's daughter took Moses to the royal palace to live with her there. What a wonderful answer to prayer!

God loves to answer our prayers, so don't be afraid to pray. Pray about everything – big things and small things. And don't forget to say thank you when God answers your prayers.

Dear God, thank you for giving Moses a good home. Help me to pray every day about the things that matter to me. Thank you that you always hear my prayers. Amen.

8 Just what you need

The king's daughter said to the mother, 'Take this baby and feed him for me. I'll pay you to take care of him.'
Exodus 2:9 (Full reading Exodus 2:9,10)

When babies are little they can't do anything for themselves. Babies need to be looked after – feeding, nappy changing and washing. The king's daughter asked Moses' mother to do all those things for Moses. Of course, Moses' mother knew exactly what Moses needed. She looked after him really well.

God wants us to know him as our heavenly Father. God knows everything about us. He knows exactly what we need. So we can trust him for all the things we need day by day.

In your prayers today, talk to God about any needs you, your friends or your family might have.

9 A bad mistake

 Moses grew and became a man ... One day Moses saw an Egyptian man beating a Hebrew man. Moses looked around and saw that no one was watching. Then Moses killed the Egyptian and buried him in the sand.

Exodus 2:11,12 (Full reading Exodus 2:11–14)

 Moses was brought up by the king's daughter, so he was like a prince of Egypt. But he knew he was really an Israelite. It must have been hard for him to see one of his own people being beaten by an Egyptian man. He was angry, so he killed the man. It was the wrong thing to do – a very bad mistake.

We all make mistakes sometimes. When we do, we need to say sorry to the person we have upset and say sorry to God.

 Dear God, I am sorry for the mistakes I have made, for the things I have said and done that upset you. Please forgive me. Amen.

10 Running away

Pharaoh heard about what Moses did, so he decided to kill Moses. But Moses ran away from Pharaoh. Moses went to the land of Midian. Moses stopped near a well in Midian.

Exodus 2:15 (Full reading Exodus 2:14,15)

Moses was afraid. People had found out about him killing the man. The king of Egypt wanted to kill Moses. So Moses decided to run away. It was the only thing he could think of doing. Moses was desperate!

When people are desperate they sometimes do silly things. They need help and prayer. If you know someone who is afraid or has big problems, pray for them today.

Dear God, you can do anything. Please take away my friend's fear and give them peace. Please stop them from doing anything silly or dangerous. Amen.

11 A helping hand

There was a priest in Midian who had seven daughters. Those girls came to that well to get water for their father's sheep ... But there were some shepherds there who chased the girls away and would not let them get water. So Moses helped the girls and gave water to their animals.
Exodus 2:16,17 (Full reading Exodus 2:16–19)

To get water in those days, you had to walk to a well – a hole in the ground where there was water. You couldn't just turn on a tap.

The girls were trying to get water for the sheep but the shepherd boys kept chasing the girls away. They needed help. So Moses helped them.

Is there someone you know who needs some help? Perhaps you could help them and make them happy.

Lord Jesus, please show me someone who needs a helping hand from me today. Amen.

12 Making good choices

 So Reuel [the priest] said to his daughters, 'Where is this man? Why did you leave him? Go invite him to eat with us.'
Exodus 2:20 (Full reading Exodus 2:18–21)

 We have now seen that Moses did one really bad thing – he killed a man – and one good thing – he helped the girls to get water. After doing the bad thing people were angry and Moses had to run away. When Moses helped the girls everybody was happy.

It is not always easy to choose good things. We need God's help to know what are the right things to do each day.

 Dear God, please help me to be wise and make good choices so the things I do will please you and put a smile on people's faces. Amen.

13 Moses settles down

Moses was happy to stay with that man. Reuel let Moses marry his daughter, Zipporah. Zipporah became pregnant and had a son.
Exodus 2:21,22 (Full reading Exodus 2:20–22)

Moses found people and a place that he liked. He had a good steady job looking after the sheep. He got married and started a family. Things were going well for Moses.

It is good for us to think about what is going well in our lives. As some people say, we should 'count our blessings'.

In your prayers today think about the place where you are living, and the people around you. Thank God for your home and your friends. Thank God for your family and your church. God is good. So count your blessings and thank him!

14 God hears our prayers

 A long time passed and that king of Egypt died. But the people of Israel were still forced to work very hard. They cried for help, and God heard them.
Exodus 2:23 (Full reading Exodus 2:23–25)

 The people of Israel were being treated very badly by the Egyptians. They were made to work very hard. The Israelites cried out to God for help. God heard their prayers and had a plan to help them.

God hears your prayers too. If you pray on your own or with other people, God hears your prayers. If you pray aloud or silently, he hears. If you pray in church, at home or on the bus, God hears.

 Thank God that he always hears you. Pray for someone by name who needs God's help. Why not talk to that friend about asking for God's help? Tell them that God hears and answers prayers.

15 God speaks to us

The Lord saw Moses was coming to look at the bush. So God called to Moses from the bush. God said, 'Moses, Moses!' Moses said, 'Yes, Lord.'
Exodus 3:4 (Full reading Exodus 3:1–6)

It must have been really scary for Moses. He was in the desert with his sheep when suddenly God spoke to him out of a burning bush. He knew it was God.

God speaks to us today. You might not hear a voice like Moses did. God can speak to you through the words of the Bible. He might use the words of a worship song to speak to you. God might use another person to speak to you, to help you understand something or to make you feel better.

Dear God, please help me to listen quietly so I will know what you are saying to me today. Amen.

16 Excuses, excuses

... Moses said to God, 'I am not a great man! How can I be the person to go to Pharaoh and lead the people of Israel out of Egypt?' God said, 'You can do it because I will be with you!'
Exodus 3:11,12 (Full reading Exodus 3:9–12)

God had a very important job for Moses. But Moses kept making excuses. Every time Moses made an excuse, God came up with a good reason why Moses should go to speak to the Pharaoh.

Sometimes we know the right thing to do, but we make excuses not to do it. Next time that happens to you, think about the answer God gave to Moses: 'I will be with you.' You need not be afraid, because God will be with you.

Dear God, please help me to know what to say to people when I am trying to do things for you. Amen.

17 You can do it!

 God said, 'You can do it because I will be with you! This will be the proof that I am sending you: After you lead the people out of Egypt, you will come and worship me on this mountain!'
Exodus 3:12 (Full reading Exodus 3:7–12)

 There it was – God's great plan. God's people were in trouble in Egypt. Moses was to go to Egypt and bring the Israelites out to a new home. Moses said he couldn't do it. 'I am not a great man', he said. But God said, 'You can do it because I am with you.'

Are you thinking, 'I can't do that!' about something you have got to do? What God said to Moses, he says to you: 'You can do it because I am with you.'

 Dear God, thank you that you are always with me, just like you were with Moses. Please give me strength and courage to do the things you want me to do. Amen.

18 With a little help

But Moses said, 'My Lord, I beg you to send another person – not me.' Then the Lord became angry with Moses and said, 'Fine! I'll give you someone to help you.'
Exodus 4:13,14 (Full reading Exodus 4:13–15)

Moses had a problem. He had to go to the king of Egypt with a message from God. But he was not a good speaker. So God sent Moses' brother Aaron to help. Moses listened to God, then Aaron would speak to the king.

We can't be good at everything. You might be good at remembering people's birthdays. But maybe you struggle with cooking. You need help from a friend with the cooking. And perhaps you can help your friend with what they find hard.

In your prayers today talk to God about the people you live with or spend a lot of time with. Pray that you can help each other so you can all enjoy a better life.

19 Speak up for God

But Pharaoh said, 'Who is the Lord? Why should I obey him? Why should I let Israel go? I don't even know who this Lord is, so I refuse to let Israel go.'
Exodus 5:2 (Full reading Exodus 5:1–5)

Moses and Aaron went to speak to Pharaoh, the king of Egypt. Pharaoh was a very important and powerful man. Moses and Aaron had to be brave to go and see him. But Pharaoh did not believe in God. Pharaoh was rude to Moses and Aaron. He told them to go away.

God wants us to tell other people about him. Those people might not believe in God yet. They might be rude to us. But they need to know that God loves them.

Pray today for a friend who does not know God. Pray that you will have a chance to talk to your friend about God soon.

20 Don't give up

 That same day, Pharaoh gave a command to make work harder for the people of Israel.
Exodus 5:6 (Full reading Exodus 5:6–9)

 Sometimes, when you pray about a problem, things get worse before they get better. That's what happened to God's people in Egypt after Moses and Aaron went to see Pharaoh. Pharaoh made the people work even harder. Things were getting worse but Moses and Aaron did not give up.

Have you been praying about something difficult, and not seen the answer to your prayer yet? Don't give up! Keep on praying and trust God to change things for the better.

 Dear God, you know everything about this problem. Please use your power to make things change.   Amen.

21 When things go wrong

So they said to Moses and Aaron, 'You really made a mistake when you told Pharaoh to let us go. May the Lord punish you because you caused Pharaoh and his rulers to hate us. You have given them an excuse to kill us.'
Exodus 5:21 (Full reading Exodus 5:19–21)

Even though Moses and Aaron were doing what God wanted, things got worse. The people of Israel turned against Moses and Aaron. So Moses cried out to God and prayed for the Israelites.

Perhaps you know what Moses felt like. Have you ever tried to help people but they turned against you? Pray for those people today.

Dear God, please help everyone to be more understanding when we want to help people and it goes wrong. Help us to live in peace together. Amen.

22 Thousands of frogs

So Aaron raised his hand over the waters of Egypt, and the frogs began coming out of the water and covered the land of Egypt.
Exodus 8:6 (Full reading Exodus 8:1–6)

Just imagine what it would be like. Frogs in the kitchen, frogs in the bathroom, in the bedroom, even in your bed! God sent the frogs when Moses lifted up his stick. Then when Moses prayed, the frogs all died. It was a sign of God's power. But even then Pharaoh did not do what God wanted. Pharaoh was very stubborn. It took him a long time to change his mind.

It takes some people a long time to believe in Jesus. You might need to talk to them lots of times before they believe. It is important to keep praying that God will change their hearts and minds.

Dear God, I pray again for my friend (say their name) to know you. Amen.

23 Help for farmers

The locusts ate every plant on the ground and all of the fruit in the trees that the hail had not destroyed.
Exodus 10:15 (Full reading Exodus 10:13–15)

After the frogs, there were other plagues. The cows and sheep died. Then the people got ill. After that there was a really bad hail storm. Then insects called locusts came. The locusts ate everything in the fields.

Even now farmers have problems with insects. The farmers sometimes have to spray their fields to keep the insects off. Being a farmer can be a hard life. They often have difficult problems to solve.

In your prayers today thank God for farmers and for the food they grow for us to eat. Pray for the men and women who work in the countryside. Pray that God will keep them safe and make their crops grow.

24 The last plague

Moses said to the people, 'The Lord says, "At midnight tonight, I will go through Egypt, and every firstborn son in Egypt will die ... But none of the people of Israel will be hurt ... " '
Exodus 11:4,7 (Full reading Exodus 11:4–7)

In the last of the plagues or disasters, the oldest boy in every Egyptian family was killed. The Israelite families put blood from a lamb over their doors. No one from the Israelite families died. They were saved because of the blood of the lambs.

This story makes us think about Jesus. Jesus died on the cross so that we can be forgiven for the things we have done wrong. We can join God's family. Because of Jesus' blood we can be saved.

Dear Lord Jesus, thank you dying on the cross for me. Please forgive me for the things I do wrong. I praise you that I can belong to God's family. Amen.

25 The great escape

The people of Israel went through the sea on dry land. The water was like a wall on their right and on their left.
Exodus 14:22 (Full reading Exodus 14:21–24)

This is one of the most famous stories in the Bible. The Egyptian army was chasing the Israelites. God pushed the water away so the Israelites could walk through the middle of the sea to a safe place. All the men in the Egyptian army were killed.

The Israelites followed God's direction and he kept them safe. It is important for us to follow God's direction. We should go where God leads us and do what God says. If we do that, God will protect us and lead us to a safe place.

Dear God, please send your Holy Spirit to help me to do the things you want me to do. Amen.

26 Our daily bread

Then the Lord said to Moses, 'I will cause food to fall from the sky. This food will be for you to eat. Every day the people should go out and gather the food they need that day.'
Exodus 16:4 (Full reading Exodus 16:4,31)

The Israelites didn't have to worry about the Egyptian army any more. But now they had another problem – no food! So God put food on the ground all round their camp. The Israelites just had to go and collect it. The Israelites didn't know what it was so they called the food 'manna'. 'Manna' means 'what is it?'

In the Lord's Prayer we say, 'Give us today our daily bread.' If we trust him, God will give us the food and other things we need each day.

Dear God, thank you for your goodness. Thank you for giving me the things I need every day. Amen.

27 No complaining

But the people were very thirsty for water. So they continued complaining to Moses. The people said, 'Why did you bring us out of Egypt? Did you bring us out here so that we, our children, and our cattle will all die without water?'
Exodus 17:3 (Full reading Exodus 17:1–3)

It seemed like the Israelites were never happy. There was always something to complain about. This time it was the water.

Some people seem to be arguing or complaining all the time. Nothing is ever good enough. And it is always somebody else's fault!

If you know somebody like that, pray for them today. Pray that they will be content or happy with what they have, and not always be wanting more.

Dear God, please help the people where I live or work to get on well together. Please stop any arguing and complaining. Amen.

28 The ten rules

Then God said, 'I am the Lord your God. I led you out of the land of Egypt where you were slaves. So you must obey these commands.'
Exodus 20:1,2 (Full reading 20:1–17)

The Ten Commandments are rules to help God's people live well. Moses went up to a mountain called Sinai to meet God and came back with the commandments on pieces of flat stone.

This happened a very long time ago, but the Ten Commandments are still important for us today.

When Jesus spoke about these commandments he said, 'You must love the Lord your God. You must love him with all your heart, all your soul, and all your mind,' and 'You must love other people the same as you love yourself' (Matthew 22:37–39).

Dear God, help me to understand what the commandments mean. Help me to keep your rules and live a better life. Amen.

29 Worship

Then the cloud covered the Meeting Tent and the Glory of the Lord filled the Holy Tent.
Exodus 40:34 (Full reading Exodus 40:33–35)

Moses set up a tent for God with special things in it. He went there to meet with God and God spoke to him.

When we go to church, the idea is to meet God and spend time with him. We meet with other Christians and worship together. These things are good for us and God will speak to us and make us stronger in our faith.

Dear God, please help the leaders of my church to know the right things to say and do. When the church meets together, please speak to us. Amen.

30 End of the journey

 The Lord said to Moses, 'This is the land I promised to Abraham, Isaac and Jacob. I said to them, 'I will give this land to your descendants ... '
Deuteronomy 34:4 (Full reading Deuteronomy 34:1–4)

 By this time Moses was well over a hundred years old. He had led the Israelites through the desert for forty years. At last they were at the end of the journey. God showed Moses the Promised Land where his people would soon live. Moses had done a good job. Sometimes things were hard, but God was always with him.

If you try to please God in your life he will always be with you. God will speak to you. He will bless other people through the things you do and say.

 Father God, thank you for the life of Moses. Help me to live well every day so my life does good to other people. Amen.

Key words

Blessings   Good things God gives to people, like peace, happiness or answered prayer.

Brave   Deciding to do something even if it is hard or dangerous.

Commandments
A list of good things to do and bad things we should not do.

Courage   Being brave when doing something hard or dangerous.

Cross   A cross is two big pieces of wood in the shape of a cross. Jesus was nailed to a cross when he died.

Descendants   Someone's children or grandchildren. Everyone in the family who comes after them.

Faith   Believing that God will keep his promises.

Forgive   When you forgive someone who has hurt you, you're not cross with them any more.

Glory   A special sign of God being there or of his power.

Hebrew   Another word for Israelite.

Holy Spirit   The Holy Spirit is a person. He is God at work on the earth.

Jew/Jewish   Belonging to the religion of the Jews. Jews believe in the God of the Old Testament. They do not believe that Jesus is the Son of God.

Peace   Quiet, calm, not worrying.

Plague   Something bad (like an illness) that affects a lot of people.

Praise   To tell God (or a person) how good they are.

Promised Land   When Abraham went to Canaan, God promised to give that land to Abraham's family.

Protect   To look after or keep safe.

Save   To rescue, set free or keep safe.

Soul   The spiritual part of a person.

Trust   Believing that someone will do what they say.

Unfair   If someone gets more than their share or if they get punished for something they didn't do, that's unfair.

Wise   A wise person always knows the right thing to do or say.

Worship   Telling God how much you love him through words or songs or things you do.

Notes for carers and helpers

These Bible guides are designed to help a wide range of people who need extra help. It's impossible to tailor Bible notes to fit everyone's needs. But our hope is that many who have some level of visual or intellectual disability or just need a simpler approach can be helped to pray and read the Bible regularly through this series.

Some people will be able to use these notes without any help from others. But if you are the carer or helper of someone needing some assistance with using them, here are a few pointers which may be useful to you.

Before you begin, ask the Holy Spirit to help communicate the main thought from each reading and note to the person you are reading with. God through the Holy Spirit can communicate on levels that we cannot! Part of the Holy Spirit's role is to make Jesus real to people and you are working in partnership with him.

Make sure you have the person's full attention before starting to read. Think about how you can eliminate auditory or visual distractions in the environment such as TV or other people's conversations. Try to find a quiet place. Use eye contact to maintain good connection.

Read slowly and clearly, pausing where suitable. Facial expressions, hand and body movements can all help to underline the meaning of the material. Encourage whatever response is appropriate, particularly in prayer and praise.

Use your knowledge of the person to assess how much is being understood, how much clarification might be needed and how best to make applications more relevant.

Make your time together an opportunity for learning and fellowship for both of you.

Other titles in the Bible Prospects series:

Being like Jesus

God gives new life

In the beginning

The first Christians

Songs of praise

The story of Christmas

The story of Easter

Bible Prospects on audio A number of these titles are available as audio CDs by mail order from Causeway PROSPECTS PO Box 351, Reading, RG30 4XQ. Phone 0118 9516 978. Email causeway@prospects.org.uk

Scripture Union produces a wide range of Bible reading notes for people of all ages and Bible-based material for small groups. SU publications are available from Christian bookshops. For information and to request free samples and a free catalogue of Bible resources:

✧   phone SU's mail order line: local rate number 08450 706006

✧   email info@scriptureunion.org.uk

✧   fax 01908 856020

✧   log on to www.scriptureunion.org.uk

✧   write to SU Mail Order, PO Box 5148, Milton Keynes MLO, MK2 2YX